SEVEN ESSENTIAL SKILLS TO SUCCESS

A POWERFUL BOOK FOR STUDENTS TO EXCEL IN LIFE, GROW FAST, BOOST CONFIDENCE AND CONQUER CHALLENGES.

PRADIP N DAS

Table of Contents

Introduction

"You can never solve a problem on the level on which it was created." — Albert Einstein

Allen and Mike were students of the same school in second grade. They went to school by the same school bus, stayed in the same locality, and played together in the same park nearby. As time passed, they became very good friends. Allen's dad, Jacob, and Mike's dad, Henry, also got to know each other and became close friends.

Once, Jacob and Henry were sitting together in the park while their children played, and they began discussing the issues they were facing in their professional and day to day life. Henry worked in a finance company whereas Jacob worked in a logistics company. Henry told Jacob that he had a lot of ambitions in life but certain things prevented him from growing. Jacob was surprised, and asked him "What problems?" Henry said that he lacks public speaking ability and communicational skills that his job demands. In his childhood, he had never paid any attention to these things. Despite his best efforts, he was not able to improve now, and that has restricted his professional growth. Jacob agreed with Henry and said that although he himself can communicate effectively, he lacks other skills such as analytical skills and is bad at writing. Both are convinced that these are learnable skills but the best time to have acquired these was their young age. In school and college, it is easy to acquire any skill, but later in life, it always becomes challenging due to many personal as well as professional commitments.

What Will Happen?

They introspected, and thought, what if the same thing happened to their children? What if, later on, they also faced similar difficulties in their professional life? They became really worried about their future. Henry said, "Something needs to be done for their skill development, and we can't ignore it". After discussing at length, they decided to take professional help. Suddenly, Jacob said, "I once met a person named David when he visited my office a few months ago, who is a mentor in skill development and a very learned person". "Wow! We should immediately contact David and take his advice", Henry said. The next day in office, Jacob searched out the contact of David and spoke to him about their problem. He called him to discuss everything he and his friend Henry were facing. David could hear Jacob's voice breaking, and he sensed how worried they were about their children's future. David listened very attentively and then suggested, "Let's have a meeting to discuss the details in person". Jacob invited them to the park.

David's Advice

Henry and Jacob explained the problem they were facing due to lack of adequate skills in their professional life. But, they were more concerned about helping their children, Allen and Mike. David listened very attentively to both Henry and Jacob and finally agreed to help them. He decided to explain in depth about skills. David said that it's a long process that requires a lot of persistence, determination, will power, and may demand sacrifices during these golden days to bring benefits in the future. The more they sharpened their skills, the more confident the children would be as they grew up.

What Are Skills?

David explained to them what skills are. He said, "Skills are nothing but our supporting weapons which help to protect, support, grow and make us successful." He further added, "Skills make a person independent, enhance self-reliance, self-esteem, reduce stress, increase confidence and help one to stand out in the crowd, and ultimately make them successful in life".

Skills are incredibly powerful, and if an individual learns even one important skill properly, he or she can earn a livelihood and excel in life.

Why Are Skills Needed?

David said, "The problem is that people do not realize the immediate benefits of learning any skill. They only realize the value of skills when they face challenges later on. On realizing this, they are hurt initially and might even try learning a skill, and sometimes they might even try learning a skill. But most people discontinue learning due to several other priorities. This cycle continues for a long time. As they grow up, acquiring these skills becomes difficult day by day. They feel the difference of not having the right skills, but by that time it is too late to compensate for the lack. Nothing left but to repent why they did not learn those essential skills at an early age. Throughout life, they ultimately pay the price for it." This way David continued explaining the different aspects of skills.

What are the basic skills required to develop in childhood itself?

A baby is not born with skills. But with time, they acquire one skill after another. The skills learned in childhood itself constitute basic communication, especially speaking and writing. Other important skills which we should learn during primary and secondary education are problem solving skills, analytical skills, and leadership skills. Negotiation skills and decision-making skills can be learned later on.

Slowly, Jacob, Henry, and David became friends. They regularly met at different places and discussed various things. Both Jacob and Henry were eager to learn the pearls of wisdom from David.

In continuation, David shared a story of two young boys aged around 12 years who were quite similar. Both enjoyed playing baseball.

And both, as it turned out, had gone to the same well-regarded secondary school. But there was a difference. One of the boys had become overwhelmed by stress and worry. He had lost his self-confidence and motivation and his school results reflected this.

The other boy found that, although the secondary school years were challenging and stressful, he was able to cope with the challenges and stress. He worked hard and achieved results that tested his true potential.

Have you ever wondered what makes this kind of difference in children's lives?

It isn't just intelligence or natural ability. It isn't that one child wants to succeed and the other does not.

The difference lies in the coping skills and mindset each child learns early on and how this shapes their experience as they tackle life's daily challenges.

In short, one boy was more resilient than the other.

They continued their discussion on skill. Jacob and Henry were very eager to understand more about skills from David so that they could guide their children.

Public Speaking Skills

What is Public Speaking Skills?

"People will forget what you said, people will forget what you did, but people will never forget how you made them feel." – Maya Angelou

What is Public Speaking Skills?

One Sunday afternoon, Henry rang David, "What are you doing today, can we meet somewhere?" David said, "Hey! Today, I'm going to City Mall where a children's speaking competition will be organized in the evening and I am one of the panel judges. By the way, if you wish, you can also join me there". Henry happily agreed to join and took Jacob also to the City Mall.

They met David outside the city mall as the competition was yet to be started. In the meantime, David explained to them about public speaking. He said, "Public speaking is a soft skill that requires subject knowledge, presentation skill, body movements, enthusiasm, and the ability to speak naturally." He paused and said, "When you can do this, the audience will enjoy your speech and your objective will be achieved."

Each individual faces public speaking in his or her daily life. Public speaking does not mean only speaking in front of thousands of people or large gatherings. Even, if you are speaking in front of a small group comprising of 2-3 persons, it is public speaking. It can be at the office during a conversation with colleagues, during a meeting, seminar, job interview, workshop, or even in interactions with juniors and seniors. Only in the case when you talk with someone very close to you, or with someone who is your friend and with whom you do not want to achieve any specific goal, it is not public speaking.

Even when you do not have any person in front of you but are speaking on camera, it is public speaking. This is because you are talking to anyone who will ever see the recording and by which you want to achieve some goal.

Why Is Public Speaking Important?

Both Jacob and Henry asked David, "What makes public speaking so important in life? What difference does it make, if somebody does not have this skill?"

David said "I remember, during my initial public speaking, when I was called to stand up and speak, I used to become so self-conscious, so nervous, that I couldn't think, couldn't concentrate, couldn't remember what I had intended to say". It is very essential to get thoughts together in a logical order. But slowly, I learned various tools and techniques associated with this skill.

Public speaking skills are of huge and crucial importance in the process of building our place in society, our professional career, even in personal relations. No matter how much you know today, you are required to learn and master the techniques of public speaking. It will help you to change your current situation, to begin to look different in the eyes of your peers, to advance in your job, to better yourself in your job, or to achieve better results and so on. Whatever your job is, you need to master the art of public speaking.

Therefore, everyone must learn public speaking skills. Whether you are in business, politics, media, whether you are a professor or a manager, or retailer, whether your goal is to act and speak in front of crowds, inboards meeting, or sales presentations to groups or individuals, or better position yourself in society, or just to be liked by someone at a coffee shop, or to appease your professor to give you a passing grade—

mastering the techniques of public speaking and oratory skills is what will make a key difference between your success or failure. In other words, when you master the techniques of public speaking, you find a better way to reach your audience.

Once you acquire this particular skill, you will be able to work easily, productive, effective, and praiseworthy. This simple skill makes all the difference in life. Like any other skill, public speaking is a learnable skill. You learn notes to learn singing, you learn steps to learn dancing. Similarly, you need to learn some tools and techniques to acquire the public speaking skills.

If you have the fear of water, you must jump into water to get rid of the fear. You have to train yourself to remove the fear, but the only way to do that is to face the fear. Similarly, if you have fear of heights, how you will get rid of this fear? Of course, the only way to get rid of the fear of height is to face the height. Similarly, if you have fear of public speaking the only way to get rid of the fear of public speaking is to face the public.

Mark Twain once famously said, "There are only two types of speakers in the world. The nervous and the liars". The truth is, we all have a fear of public speaking. Some have less fear, others more. However, by learning a few basic tools and techniques and religiously practicing, you can improve and master the public speaking skills and deliver good speeches.

Public speaking is an art; and, like every other art, it has to be learned, both in practice and in theory. For a man to say that he will never deliver a speech until he has learned to speak is like saying that he will never go into the water until he has learned to swim.

How to Learn Public Speaking

There is a saying that the expert in anything was once a beginner. One cannot learn soccer without going to the field, and one can never learn to speak in public without getting up on stage. In both cases, one has to learn by practice; and no amount of theory without practice will be of any use.

Albert Mehrabian, Professor Emeritus of Psychology at the University of California, Los Angeles, developed a communication model, in which he demonstrated that only 7% of what we communicate consists of the literal content of the message. The use of one's voice, such as tone, intonation, and volume, takes up 38%, and as much as 55% of communication consists of body language.

In public speaking, the management of the voice is very important. Some speakers speak too softly and cannot be heard well in a large hall. Some are too loud, but the echo drowns their voices. Some talk so fast that they cannot be followed; and some speak so slowly as to tire their listeners' patience. The speaker should speak clearly and naturally. Some voice modulation can be done to stress on certain parts of the speeches and the person should also know when to make effective pauses.

There are a few important things which can help to improve public speaking.

- Strong & Effective Start

  You should start a presentation in such a way that you catch the attention of the audience immediately. The best speeches grab you from the first moment and never let you go. There are some modern tools and techniques for starting any presentation. You should act normal, smile, and be confident. You can start with a story or incidents or research articles or quotes and connect that the topic you are going to deliver.

- Make great content

The content is the most important in any presentation. Content is the key, but it should be organized in such a way that the audience should not feel overburdened with an ocean of information. You should plan the content in a concise, to the point manner, structured in a way to engage the audience all the time.

- Body movement

The body parts that play a decisive role in effective speaking are eyes, hands, legs, shoulders, and mouth.

Your hand should not be inside the pocket or behind your back. It should be in an open gesture position or steeple hand method.

The legs can either be cemented in one position or can be moved with control. The rhythmic movements of legs are a sign of nervousness.

You should make direct eye contact with the audience, should smile, and keep your shoulders straight.

- Voice management

When you speak in a natural voice, the connection with the audience automatically builds. Your voice should be clear and audible to the audience. It should not be too fast or too slow. Pauses are important in between. You can stress on certain points or words just to emphasize the importance.

- Powerful closing

Closing a speech is very important. Your conclusion is delivered at the end of the speech and is often what most people remember immediately after your speech has ended. As important as your introduction is for grabbing the audience's attention, the conclusion is doubly important as it leaves the audience with a lasting impression. Just as an introduction can make or break a speech, you always want to end your speech on a high note with something memorable. The conclusion is where you can insert your take-away message. What do you want the audience to remember after you have finished speaking? What do you want them to recall in the days or weeks after your speech?

To create a memorable ending, you may want to share a quotation or reconfirm the promises made at the beginning of the speech. You can summarize the speech with important points. You need to be sure to craft your conclusion in a way that is still appropriate to the topic, audience, and venue.

- Practice as if it's the last opportunity

There's a good reason to say, "Practice makes perfect!" You simply cannot be a confident, compelling speaker without practice. To get practice, seek opportunities to speak in front of others. If you will deliver a presentation or speech, create it as early as possible. The earlier you put it together, the more time you will have to practice.

You need to practice as much as you can. Try making videos with your mobile phone and then analyzing them carefully in terms of content, vocal management, body movements, etc. After analyzing, work on those areas where you need improvement, continue the same process repeatedly until it reaches to your satisfaction level.

Chapter Summary

To conclude, public speaking is one form of communication to influence others. It is very important in our life regardless of educational background or profession. Preparation is very important as it increases the effectiveness of the speech and leads to a successful performance.

"An effective speaker knows that the success or failure of his talk is not for him to decide—it will be decided in the minds and hearts of his hearers." - Dale Carnegie

Important Points to Note

- Public speaking is a learnable skill. Tools and techniques of public speaking need to be learned to get ahead in life.

- For effective public speaking, you have to set objectives, do preparation related to the start, the content, and the end.

- Delivery of the content is very important. So, you need to learn the body movements and vocal management which together constitute 93% of the effectiveness of public speaking.

- Finally, practice is a must to enhance this skill.

Writing Skills

"There is no greater agony than bearing an untold story inside you." - Maya Angelou

What Are Writing Skills?

"What are you doing nowadays?" Henry asked David. He replied "I am reading 'The Writer's Choice' a book by Anne Janzer. A great book to improve writing ability."

"Do you write, David?" Jacob asked. "Yes, I am not a professional writer, but I write something every day. This is a good book to improve your writing", said David.

Henry asked, "I don't understand how they write long books? Can it be learned?" David replied, "Writing is one such skill which people wish to learn, but most of them do not succeed because they want quick success." He added, "It requires years of learning, practice, correcting and improving. A good reader can learn quickly about writing. Writing comes with flow and flow comes with ideas. Writing means getting the idea, organizing it, and putting it on the paper." They kept on discussing writing, why it is important, how it can be learned, etc.

Writing is the ability to express ideas through the written word. In any organization, the ability to communicate ideas through writing is in high demand. Properly written documents, emails, and posts can persuade customers to purchase a product or convince investors to partner with a company. Good project documents, proposals, emails, technical documents, formatting of documents for different situations, etc. require good writing skills. The writing style and the tone based on the situation are important writing skills that matter.

Importance of Writing Skills

Writing skills are an essential part of communication. Good writing skills allow you to communicate your message with clarity, precision, and ease. One can reach a much larger audience through writing than through speaking. Every organization needs employees with good writing abilities so that the opinions, thoughts, and ideas are communicated to the stakeholders properly and as intended. Writing skills thereby allow you to maintain clear communication and accurate documentation in any workplace.

Besides good command of the language, writing requires a good understanding of the reader; once you understand their requirements, you will be able to write effectively.

Writing does not require the sender or the receiver of the message to be at same place or time. Writing skills allow you to communicate clearly with others and create useful resources for the workplace.

How to Improve Writing Skills?

Jacob was quietly listening when suddenly he asked David, "Tell us how to improve our writing skills?" David said, "In short, writing skills are improved by reading, learning, and writing."

David continued, "Once you master this skill, you can separate yourself from the masses and stand out. If you read great writers, you will understand the incredible ways in which they turn ideas into words.

While some people are naturally talented in writing, anyone can develop their writing skills over time. Once you understand the different types of writing skills, you can focus on how to use them in the workplace and improve over time. Identify your strongest writing skills and develop strategies to improve those skills to a professional level.

- Read daily

Just as listening is related to speaking, reading is related to writing. The first important point to remember for improving writing is to read as much as you can. Reading improves vocabulary, grammar, sentence structure, and shows different ways to communicate ideas. It also stimulates critical thinking on any subject. By reading, you get to know how these great writers use their words and write sentences. All these will help you develop your writing skills. When you study different types of writing and literature, you will understand the use of words, the flow of sentences, and how the author hooks the readers through his or her experiences.

The best writers are also keen readers, and reading regularly is an easy way to start developing your writing skills.

- Learn grammar and vocabulary

Grammar is the basis of any language. If you want to have command in any language, the fundamental requirement is grammar. Remember that grammar is more important when you write than when you speak, because writing is usually more formal and more structured. Good knowledge of grammar not only makes you a better writer, but it also helps you to be a more productive writer. Grammar makes a piece of writing effective because it bridges the gap between the reader's understanding and the communicator's intent.

Second, the bigger the word bank, the easier it is to write without interruption. Part of becoming a better writer is learning new words. So, while reading, you should be looking for words and phrases that could be useful when writing about the topics that interest you.

- Make a Habit to Write Daily

How did Michael Jordon improve his basketball? By playing basketball. How did Messi or Ronaldo improve their football? By playing football. So, if you wish to get better at something, you have to practice, and writing is no exception. The best way to improve writing is to write every day and analyze the same. It improves with practice and the more you write, the better you will become. There is no other way. You need to practice writing to become a better writer.

"Start writing, no matter what. The water does not flow until the faucet is turned on." - Louis L'Amour

Chapter Conclusion

Writing is a very important skill that should be practiced and acquired from early age. By writing, you share your knowledge, your experience, and your views to millions of people.

In general, writing improves personality. When you become a good writer, you earn respect, and people follow you. Hence writing skills are very important. Whether you are a student or an employee, writing skills help you in every field.

Writing is an extremely complex cognitive activity in which the writer is required to demonstrate control of multiple variables simultaneously. Strong writing skills may enhance students' chances of success. Good writing skills are needed for all students to accomplish their educational and professional requirements.

Important Points to Note

- The best way to improve writing skills is to read, read and read.

- Writing every day is a must to create habit.

- Reviewing or analyzing your writing is necessary to understand improvement areas.

- To improve writing skills, focus on strengthening your word power and grammar

Analytical Skills

"My father used to say 'Don't raise your voice, improve your argument.'" – Desmond tutu

What Are Analytical Skills?

Day by day, Henry kept becoming more curious about skills. He asked David, "I heard about analytical skills. What is that and how one can improve it?"

David paused for a moment and asked Jacob, "Do you also want to know about analytical skills? Jacob nodded.

They went to a nearby restaurant, sat in an open space, and ordered snacks, tea, and coffee. David then started explaining the basics of analytical skills, its importance, and how to improve it.

David said, "Let me share a real story that happened to me."

He continued "I started my career by working with a research and development institute. After a few days of joining, I encountered a herculean task: I was given all the customer feedback related to telecommunication. There were about twenty questionnaires, subjective as well as objective. I had to analyze all customer feedback data within a week. I was puzzled and confused. "How will I start the work? How will I do that?" One of my colleagues sensed my problem and came forward to assist me. He taught me several ways of analyzing the data. Then, realizing the importance of analytical skills and knowing that these are tasks that I could face in the future too, I joined a course on data handling and analysis. There I learned many new things such as extracting findings from large data.

This skill is very important, so let us first understand what analytical skills are.

Analytical skills allow you to collect, gather, visualize, and analyze information in detail. This includes the ability to see a problem or situation from various perspectives. Analytical skills allow you to solve complex problems by making decisions most effectively.

Analytical thinking refers to observing complex problems and synthesizing information to develop approaches to resolve or further explore them.

Why Are Analytical Skills Important?

Analytical skills are very important because they allow you to find solutions to common problems and help in making decisions for the next actions. Understanding problems and analyzing the situation for viable solutions is a key skill in every position, every level. Developing this ability can improve your work, help you achieve company goals, and eventually support your personal career goals.

Analytical skills are not just required for data analysts or accountants. If you're looking for a career in finance, marketing, operations, or even for your own business, analytical skills are essential.

In a world of fierce competition and dynamic markets, it is essential to understand data because data speaks a lot. Analytical skills are critical for budgeting, competitor analysis, customer feedback, campaign performance, financial status, strategic planning, and so on.

If you want to get more output at work, then you need to master analytical thinking. Analytical thinking is a powerful skill that helps in detecting patterns, brainstorming, observing, interpreting data, and making decisions based on the multiple factors and options available to you.

How to Improve Analytical Skills

- Read more

  A good way to start improving your analytical skills is through the power of the written word. Reading stimulates your thinking and broadens your imagination. Reading boosts analytical thinking. Readers improve their general knowledge and can spot patterns quicker than non-readers. Indeed, the more you expose yourself to different ideas, the more you'll increase your cognitive abilities. Therefore, the key to improving your analytical thinking skills is to keep your mind active and running.

- Listen more

There are excellent podcasts such as Developer Tea, Broken Brain, and TED Radio Hour, which will give you useful tips for stimulating creativity and challenging your thoughts and ideas, ultimately helping you enhance your mental capacity.

- Play mind games

Playing mind games such as Sudoku, Chess, crossword puzzles and Scrabble can expand your critical thinking. Even fifteen minutes a day of playtime can increase your mental stimulation and improve your analytical skills.

This is a good way to improve your analytical skills and brainpower. Brain games challenge one to think deeply and logically, which are often a preferred method used to sharpen analytical skills.

It's a great way to develop their analytical skills while having fun.

- Learn every day

Often after graduating from high school or university, most people become passive in matters of learning new things. Indeed, learning more no longer remains a priority once you've advanced into the professional world, but that doesn't mean that you should stop expanding your knowledge. Instead, You should try to learn something new every day: it could be about your particular field, your finances in general, or personal issues like health.

- Be observant

When you're observant, you tend to notice more around you, and this sparks your critical thinking. Paying attention to detail and being observant is a great way to improve your analytical skills because it allows you to process the way things work and interact. Using your senses and actively engaging in the world around you will help you hone your analytical skills.

The key to improving your analytical thinking skills is to be open and to constantly challenge yourself to learn more. Once you do that, you will be able to comprehend and appreciate debates and concepts, break down complex information, and streamline solution-finding processes.

- Take an online course

If you do have time for education, then taking an online course can be a great way to develop your analytical skills. Try to take courses about subjects in which you aren't very familiar or good. For example, not many people are good at Excel, but with time and dedication, you can master the use of formulas and cells and become an Excel expert yourself. The point is to expand your knowledge and challenge yourself with topics you don't have any prior experience in.

- Ask questions

Curiosity drives us to be more motivated, intelligent, and creative. The questions that we ask ourselves force us to reconsider our old thoughts and come to a logical solution.

When someone asks questions, they're often looking for clarification and understanding. Expressing curiosity provides you with different perspectives and allows you to compare your own opinion with someone else's. Sometimes your questions will lead you to a different answer than initially expected. So, the more knowledge you soak in, the better your analytical skills will become.

- Physical Exercise

  Believe it or not, exercise can also aid in the development of your analytical thinking skills. Exercising more frequently can help improve your cognitive abilities. In exercise classes, memorizing the next steps in a workout routine is a great way to help develop your analytical skills. Knowing the sequence will help keep you focused on the task at hand while also helping you prepare for what's next.

- Keep a diary

  Keeping a diary has many benefits. It helps you reflect on your day, it forces you to analyze your actions and learn from any achievements or mistakes. Besides, it helps in improving your mental health and your ability to process difficult experiences. Writing regularly in a personal learning journal can be an effective way to develop critical thinking skills.

Chapter Summary

"Thank you, David, for helping us to learn about analytical skills," Jacob said. "Let me summarize what we have learned today", Henry said. He then continued, "This skill is really important and can become a useful tool in professional life. We can learn and improve analytical skills by reading, observing, learning, asking questions, by keeping a diary and by taking professional courses."

Important Points to Note

- Analytical skills are very important in one's professional career. Analytically skilled persons are better problem solvers.

- One can improve analytical skills by reading, learning, playing mind games, asking questions, etc.

Problem Solving Skills

"Most people spend more time and energy going around problems than in trying to solve them." - Henry Ford

What is Problem Solving Skills?

One beautiful morning, David, Jacob, and Henry were enjoying hot coffee and discussing skills. David said, "Let me share a real story."

Once while he was busy at work, his little daughter Nancy was constantly disturbing him. So, to keep her busy, he tore a page of a complex picture from a magazine and asked her to piece them together in her room. David was pretty sure that it would take her hours to get it done.

David was surprised when he saw Nancy coming out of the room within a few minutes with a smile, holding the perfect picture. He asked his daughter how she could solve the puzzle so quickly.

"Daddy, there is a woman's face on the other side of the paper. When I made the face perfectly, I got the picture right." replied the young girl.

Therefore, there is always the other side of whatever you experience in this world. Whenever we come across a challenge or a puzzling situation, look at the other side. You will be surprised to see different approaches to tackle the problem.

David presented another example. Suppose, it's a hot summer afternoon and you need to go to the medical store to take medicine for your mother. What do you do? You can take your umbrella and walk, or you can drive, or hire a car. You might call a friend for a ride, or you might postpone going to the store another day. There are a lot of possible solutions. There is no right way to solve this problem and different people will solve it differently.

David said, "You know, life is full of challenges, and problems creep up with challenges if it is not managed properly." He continued, "Problems are part and parcel of life. They always remain and those who tackle them effectively, without stress, become successful in life. You can either call it a problem or a challenge or an opportunity.

A problem is an opportunity for improvement. "Every problem has a gift for you in its hands," says Richard Bach.

Hence, a problem is something hard to understand or accomplish or deal with. It can be a task, a situation, or even a person. Problem solving involves methods and skills to find the best solutions to problems.

Why Are Problem Solving Skills Necessary?

Great People in history like Eleanor Roosevelt, Nelson Mandela, Steve Jobs, Mahatma Gandhi, Martin Luther King Jr., etc. are all great problem solvers. We all have decisions to make, situations to face, and questions to answer in our lives. The ability to solve problems is one of the basic skills and is essential to our everyday life at home, school, and workplace. We solve problems every day without really thinking about how we solve them and sometimes it can be an unconscious effort. It just happens. But, what is important is how we solve a problem, what prices we pay for it, and what impact it has.

Mastering problem solving skills is a must in today's life scenario. Many people avoid challenges as they do not like to face problems. They do not know how to handle problems and become stressed. It is essential to understand the problem solving tools and techniques to channelize their prospects.

Nevertheless, to be effective at problem solving, some other key skills have to be kept in mind that include analytical skills, communication skills, leadership skills, etc.

What Is The Process of Problem Solving?

David explains, "See, humans start learning how to solve a simple problem from a very early age, right from learning how to eat, walk, speak, run, etc." All these are skills, humans learn with their age." But if it is done in a structured way, the process becomes easier and helps one to become successful in life. The Japanese are very famous for solving problems. They have inculcated many problem solving tools in life which they practice regularly. Problem solving is a skill and these skills are learnable.

A problem solving process starts with understanding the problem and ends with eliminating the problem.

Each step in the problem solving process employs skills and methods that contribute to the overall effectiveness of influencing change and determining the level of problem complexity that can be addressed.

i) Understanding the problem: Albert Einstein once said: "The formulation of the problem is often more essential than its solution, which may be merely a matter of mathematical or experimental skill."

ii) Defining the Problem: The next step in problem solving is the ability to break down the problem into small pieces by defining the main elements of the problem. Defining the problem is a concise description of the problem to address. The problem statement identifies the current position, the desired requirement, and any gaps between the two. Identify the issue with which you're dealing. Observe the problem area closely to form a detailed image of what is wrong. This is an outwardly simple but vital step. If you don't properly understand the problem, your solutions may be ineffective or they may fail. To define the problem, you will have to ask questions and look at different angles.

iii) Brainstorming and identification of possible solutions: This is one of the most important stages of problem solving. By this process, you list down all the possible reasons causing the problem, followed by a classification of possible reasons under common head through the Ishikawa diagram or cause and effect diagram.

Brainstorming activities are very important in problem solving. The purpose here is to come up with all the possible reasons and solutions, even if they seem ridiculous at first. You must keep an open mind to boost creative thinking during brainstorming, which can trigger potential solutions. Change the 'direction' of your thoughts by thinking laterally. You can use the mind map technique.

iv) Analyze the reasons: It requires a careful balance between analytical and logical thinking. At this stage, all reasons are analyzed or investigated with the available information and tools, and we come to the actual conclusion.

v) Prepare an action plan: From a wide variety of possible solutions, you need to select the best solution to solve the problem. Strong decision-making is essential at this stage. After carefully considering all options, you must select the best strategy for your problem and stick with your choice.

vi) Implement your solution: Implementation is a critical part of the problem solving process. This is where you draw up a step-by-step execution plan, share it with the appropriate personnel, and follow through with your chosen approach. This is also an important skill as it would not matter how effectively you identify the problem, define its elements and examine possible solutions if the final implementation fails; everything boils down to the ability to perform concrete steps to execute the action plan.

vii) Evaluation: This is the final step in the problem solving process. You should review the effectiveness of the solution against desired outcomes. What went right? What went wrong? This stage requires a careful analysis that improves upon the best solution. The review of your progress can help to revise any step or new steps to be added. One may look for a different solution if the current one is not helping.

How to Improve Problem Solving Skills

There is a belief that an individual has to be very intelligent to be a good problem solver, but that is not true. Problem solving skills are important in every industry. When you're in a management position, one of the most important things you do is to handle the day-to-day issues that arise for your employees. Improving your problem solving skills will give you a distinct edge in not only a management job but also in other positions within your company. You can hone your problem solving skills by:

- Questioning

  Questioning is a great technique to understand the problem, and you will be directed to a solution. The 5Ws (Why, What, When, Who, Where) and 1H (How) clear many matters. At every step, if you ask a question, things become clearer.

- Learn problem solving tools

  There are many problem solving tools such as the Ishikawa diagram, 5 why, Pareto chart, histogram, scatter diagram, etc.

  The Ishikawa diagram or fishbone diagram is used mainly for identifying the root causes of the problem. It sorts possible causes into various categories that branch off from the original problem.

Pareto chart works with an 80/ 20 rule, where it says 80% of the problems are associated with 20% of causes, and the remaining 20% of the problems come from 80% of the causes.

A scatter diagram uses pairs of data points to find relationships between variables and to determine whether two variables are correlated.

The 5 Whys method uses a series of questions to drill down into successive layers of a problem. Each time you ask why the answer becomes the basis of the next why.

- Active listening

Active listening is one of the most important skills for problem solving. Active listening is a technique used to not only better understand what is being said by an individual, but also to be more aware of the underlying message the speaker is trying to convey.

When it comes to problem solving, active listening is integral for understanding the position of every participant and to clarify the challenges, ideas, and solutions they bring to the table. Popular active listening skills include paying complete attention to the speaker, removing distractions, avoiding interruption, making eye contact, smiling, judging the situation and responding appropriately. You can disagree without being disrespectful. You can observe body language, remain neutral, ask deeper questions based on what is said, and clarify points wherever necessary.

- Develop analytical skills

All problem solving models require strong analytical skills, particularly during the beginning of the process and when it comes to evaluating how solutions have been performed.

Analytical skills are primarily focused on performing an effective analysis by collecting, studying, and parsing data related to a problem or opportunity.

It often involves spotting patterns, being able to see things from different perspectives, and using observable facts and data to make suggestions or produce insight.

Analytical skills are also important at every stage of the problem solving process, and by having these skills, you can ensure that any ideas or solutions you create have been sufficiently thought out.

- Improve observation power

The power of observation is very important in any problem solving. A good observer easily finds clues by closely searching in the surrounding areas of the problem.

- Collaboration

Trying to solve problems on your own is difficult. Remember that irrespective of your role, collaboration is integral, and in a problem solving process, you are all working together to find the best solution. On a personal level also, the collaborative roles of the family members are important.

- Communication

Being an effective communicator means being empathetic, clear, and succinct. It means asking the right questions and demonstrating active listening skills throughout any discussion or meeting.

In any problem solving, you need to communicate well to progress through each stage of the process effectively. As a team leader, it may also fall on you to facilitate communication between parties who do not see eye to eye. Effective communication also means helping others to express themselves and be heard in a group.

- Decision-making

All problems need a solution and all solutions require someone to implement them. Without strong decision-making skills, teams can become bogged down in discussions and become less efficient as a result.

Making decisions is a key part of the problem solving process. It's important to remember that decision-making is not restricted to the leadership team. Every staff member makes decisions every day and developing these skills ensures that your team can solve problems at any scale.

Remember that making decisions does not mean leaping to the first solution but weighing up the options and coming to an informed, well thought out solution to any given problem.

- Leadership

In the problem solving process, strong leadership helps ensure that the process is efficient, that all conflicts are resolved, and that a team is managed in the direction of success.

It is important that the leader maintains impartiality and does not force the group in a particular direction. Remember that good leadership means working in service of the purpose.

Chapter Summary

In a nutshell, problem solving skill is very critical in our life and everybody should learn more of it. To improve problem solving skills, you should focus on improving learning, reading, listening, critical thinking, questioning, leadership, communication, etc.

Important Points to Note

- Understanding the problem is very important, and then follow the problem solving process.
- Learn problem solving tools and techniques such as brainstorming, 5 Why method, Ishikawa diagram, Pareto Chart, Scatter diagram, etc.
- Improve problem solving skills by reading more, active listening, observing, questing, learning effective communication, developing analytical skills, etc.

Negotiation Skills

"Negotiation in the classic diplomatic sense assumes parties more anxious to agree than to disagree." – Dean Acheson

What is Negotiation?

David, Henry, and Jacob were travelling together on a train. Just in front of their sitting row, a couple was also travelling with their teenage child. The child wanted a smartphone for himself, but his mom was unwilling to buy one for him. She was well aware of the problems caused by phones. Because the child was insisting, she agreed to put certain conditions for purchasing him a smartphone. She said, "Allen, you will get a smartphone next year only if you learn French this year." Allen did not agree initially, but his mother was firm in her stand, and he finally agreed.

David said, "This is one kind of negotiation or agreement." He continued, "Negotiation is a skill which every individual should learn. We negotiate almost every day, and if we know how to negotiate, the outcome will be in our favor in most of the cases."

Negotiation is an effort that focuses on gaining the favor of the people in the matter being discussed. It can be anything, such as money, justice, status, love, safety, security, recognition, etc. An individual who has negotiation skills can get things in their favor.

David said, "We negotiate all the time, both in our professional and personal life. An individual comes across many differences with family members, stakeholders, bosses, friends, colleagues, clients, etc. How do they handle those conflicts? How do they compromise to reach a common ground?

Why Is Negotiation Important?

Negotiation plays a significant role in daily life, particularly in the professional world. The purpose of Negotiation is to reach an agreement. In many negotiations, people can settle differences without arguing. In business transactions, disagreements are inevitable, and hence, negotiation is required to bring both parties to an agreeable position. In a negotiation process, all the players strive to have a position that best fits their interests.

For every successful business, negotiation is a major part. The art of negotiation is an essential skill in the modern era. But negotiating is not easy, as it is a trait that has to be developed.

Negotiation is important from time to time since it helps in solving conflicts and disagreements. To achieve the desired outcome, it is useful to have a structured negotiation approach. For example, in a business situation, a meeting has to be arranged for the involved parties to meet, to negotiate, and to come to an agreement. To know more about negotiation, you can read the book "You can negotiate anything" by Herb Cohen.

Negotiation Process

Henry asked, "How is negotiation done? Is there any process for it?" David said, "Let me explain to you the negotiation process from an organization's perspective."

Negotiation is a method by which people settle differences and reach an agreement through a process involving compromises, while avoiding disputes.

i) Preparation: Preparation is the first stage in any negotiation. Once the place and time are decided for negotiation, both parties start preparing for the negotiation. Preparation mainly involves gathering all the information related to the subject of negotiation, understanding the pros and cons of different situations, different questions, and counter questions, etc. Negotiators also need to set their goals during the negotiation process. Being under prepared increases the chances of conflict and wastage of time.

ii) Discussion: At this stage, members of each side present their case. Skills useful at this stage include listening, clarifying, and questioning. It is sometimes helpful to make notes for future reference and for asking questions. Listening is very important since when disagreements occur, people tend to talk too much and listen very little. All sides should have equal time and opportunity to present their case. After the discussion, interest, goals, and viewpoints of all sides should be considered. This can be listed according to priorities, which will help to identify and establish a common solution.

iii) Agreement: Each party in a negotiation seeks to win. Thus, each party needs to focus on a win-win outcome. A win-win solution should always be aimed for but this is not always possible. Because of this, you should make other backup strategies. Compromises are positive alternatives that will often accomplish more benefits than the original positions.

iv) From an agreement, a course of action is prepared and conveyed. If an agreement has not been reached, another meeting can be arranged to save time from meaningless arguments, which may also damage future business relationships. Sometimes, it is helpful to invite an outside party to mediate.

How to Improve Negotiation Skills

- Establish Objectives

  Often, an individual goes into a negotiation without a clear understanding of what exactly he or she wants and why. This is important because you need to know the limits up to which you can compromise. You will not win every negotiation, and an individual should know when to continue negotiating and when to walk away.

- Clear understanding

  Possibly the most important part of negotiating is understanding both the value of what you have to offer and the perceived value of what you are asking for in return. Remember, you are always trying to create a win-win, so you must demonstrate how what you are seeking is the best for both parties.

- Anticipate counter perspectives

  Many times, we think we know what others want, when in reality we do not. Don't make the mistake of assuming you know what the other person wants until you take the time to consider their perspective, position, experience, and reputation. Practice empathy. Not everyone is going to be upfront and honest about what they want but considering what you know can point towards a clearer picture of the reasoning behind their tactics. Being able to understand someone else's situation will enhance your communication and help steer toward the fairest, most equitable outcome.

- Aim for a win-win outcome

  Great negotiators do their best to create win-win situations but doing so involves knowing what the other person or party hopes to achieve and why. Once you know what both you and the other person or party want, you can begin the process of reaching a fair outcome. This doesn't always happen, however. Many times, hardball negotiators hide their true intentions to get you to accept what works best for them. This is where it becomes highly important for you to understand your bottom line and what you will and will not accept.

- Be strong

The negotiating party may or may not always respond politely and can sometimes become very aggressive. You should always remain calm and respectful while expressing your needs explicitly. You should be assertive. In some scenarios, it is acceptable to tell someone that their behavior is unacceptable and that you will not budge to manipulative tactics.

- Remain cool and calm

Tough negotiators can mobilize many tactics to push your buttons. It's important to maintain a calm, cool and collected demeanor even when they incite you to act emotionally. There is nothing wrong with asking to take a break to cool down if you feel the atmosphere getting heated. Remember, you cannot control their behavior or tactics, but you can control your own. A cool head will always help you get a better outcome than an emotional reaction.

- Understand the boundary

Ultimately, there are going to be people in this world with whom you cannot negotiate. Sometimes, a person might just want to see how far they can push you before you walk away. Always enter situations knowing where your "hard line" is. Sometimes, walking away will put a lid on negotiations. In other instances, however, it will communicate that you are not someone easily taken advantage of and negotiations may not only resume but also go much more smoothly.

Chapter Conclusion

To conclude, negotiation is a process by which two parties seek to reach an agreement through bargaining. A win-win negotiation situation is likely when each party is prepared to give up something to achieve something the other party has.

Negotiation process need to be followed properly to get favorable outcomes. Negotiation skills can be improved by understanding the goal, making proper strategy, asking questions, anticipating other party's perspective, etc.

Important Points to Note

- Before the negotiation, gather information, set goals, make strategy and prepare questions and counter questions.

- During the negotiation, listen properly to understand the viewpoint of the other party.

- Agreement or disagreement should be noted and signed off.

- For better results in negotiations, an individual also needs to improve analytical skills, problem solving skills, and public speaking skills.

Leadership Skills

"If your actions inspire others to dream more, learn more, do more and become more, you are a leader." – John Quincy Adams

What Are Leadership Skills?

Once Jacob and Henry were sitting with David on the lawn of the city library. They were discussing the forthcoming American presidential election. Suddenly, David said, "See, all the ex-presidents of America are great leaders." He continued, "Mr. Joe Biden and Mr. Jacob Trump are good leaders too. Irrespective of who becomes the next President, the United States should be proud of their leadership, and the country will flourish." Jacob interrupted David and asked, "What make them the great leaders?"

"See, leaders possess certain qualities. Do you want to know more about leaders and leadership skills?" David asked. Both Henry and Jacob nodded.

David said, "In today's competitive world, leadership skills are crucial for both personal and professional development. It benefits an individual or a business to flourish by maximizing efficiency and achieving goals. Leadership has different meanings for different persons. Leadership is the process of influencing the activities of a group in the setting and the achievement of goals." Henry said, "This is difficult for me to understand." David said, "Henry, It's not so difficult. Let me help you."

Why Are Leadership Skills Important?

David said, "Be it in the battlefield, or in sports, or in the corporate world, leadership is the key to success. Battles are won not only with weapons but also with the mind. A good leader can lead his army towards victory through proper planning and execution. Similarly, in sports or in business, success depends largely on leaders.

People need good leadership skills to succeed at personal, professional, and social fronts. Personal leadership helps us determine our desires, strengths, and abilities. It means knowing what we want out of life; knowing what success means for us; setting our goals and planning how to achieve them regardless of what other people think, say, or do. Personal leadership helps us to make our present better and shape our future.

Good leadership is very important for professionals to succeed. Leadership is crucial in implementing decisions correctly and successfully.

Leadership occurs in all formal and informal situations. In a non-formal situation, such as a group of friends, leadership behavior occurs when one individual takes lead in most of the group activities and influences people to work towards common goals.

The real test of leaders takes place in times of crisis. Leaders step up in these situations. They take control, analyze, communicate, persuade, help, negotiate, encourage, and do all kinds of activities required to lead the group out of the crisis.

The ability to influence the behavior of others is known as leadership. Leaders nourish talent and potential to bring out the best in everyone. Leadership is a process by which a person influences others to accomplish an objective. A leader inspires confidence and support among group members to achieve their goals.

Leadership is the process by which an executive directs, guides, and influences the work of others in choosing and attaining specified goals. Dynamic and effective leadership leads an organization to success.

A good leader is always courageous, punctual, hardworking, fluent, wise, and flexible. They lead followers using their leadership qualities. Some people are born leaders, but most others learn leadership qualities and become popular.

Leadership is the art of leading a group of people or an organization and influencing others to follow that direction. It may be defined as a position held by an individual in a group. A leader is responsible for guiding a group of employees and developing and implementing a timeline for his team to reach their goal.

Leadership Qualities or Skills

Leadership is a useful tool in most aspects of life. Leadership is a quality that can benefit family, organization, country, and the world. A good leader possesses many skills. One needs to have some unique leadership qualities and special skills to become a good leader. The question of what makes a good leader is widely debated. It is clear that the ability to lead effectively relies on several qualities:

- First of all, honesty is the foremost quality that a leader needs to be successful. A good leader should always be noble and honest. Otherwise, one cannot have followers who look up to him.

- A good leader always inspires his followers and motivates them in achieving the goal. According to John Quincy Adams, if the action of a person inspires others to dream more, learn more, do more, and become more, he is called a great leader. A great leader should always think positively and his positive approach must be visible through his actions.

- Great leaders are also great communicators. If a leader wants to get results as early as possible, he/ she must know how to communicate with his/ her team and tell them the strategy to achieve the goal. If a person doesn't know how to communicate with his/ her team members effectively, he/ she can never be a good leader. A good leader does not maintain distance from them but shares his thoughts directly.

- Patience is an important leadership quality. A person who loses his temper easily is not considered a good leader. A successful leader always keeps patience in his work.

- A great leader should be always committed and passionate about his job. A committed leader always finds value and purpose in his organization and shares that commitment with his team members. It also helps him to gain their respect and inspire them to perform better.

- An efficient leader has good decision-making capabilities and can make the right decisions at the right time. Leaders have well-developed decision-making ability and can make a perfect choice from several options.

- Confidence is one major leadership quality that can be seen in a good leader. A leader must have enough self-confidence to convince followers that they can achieve their goal.

How to Develop Leadership Skills

"A good leader takes a little more than his share of the blame, a little less than his share of credit" – Arnold H. Glasow

- **Take Ownership**

  Taking ownership is the best way to develop leadership skills. Taking initiatives and new challenges are the indicators of ownership. Always remember that stepping out of your comfort zone is the only way you will learn anything new.

- **Be Compassionate and Inspire others**

You should start motivating and inspiring all those who work with you and collaborating in the best way you can. If a team member needs encouragement or guidance, make sure that you help him.

The best way to become a great leader is to train yourself to become better and better every day and to help others learn and grow.

- **Keep learning**

You should start learning new things because learning keeps the mind sharp and fresh. It prepares you for new challenges that may come your way, which is always a good thing in a leader.

Some people indeed have inbuilt qualities and a great talent to lead others. But, for me, experience and learning also make good leaders. We learn and grow every day. If today you are learning from your leader, tomorrow you will become a leader and make others learn. A great way to develop your leadership skills is to take on more responsibility and get more experience.

- **Empower your teammates**

No one is great at everything, and the sooner you realize that the sooner you can learn to be a good leader. You should start delegating tasks to others because it not only allows you to focus on things you do well, but it also empowers other people on your team.

- **Be passionate**

  When you display authentic enthusiasm and passion for the result, your team members will keep working to achieve their goals. Employees respond to those who are eager to help them learn and grow. Show passion for everything you do, including your efforts at developing leadership skills.

- **Communicate**

  Communication is one of the most powerful tools. You can solve most problems and overcome most obstacles if you are a good communicator. A good communicator is not just a great speaker but a great listener too. It's important to keep a tab on everyone involved in your team and make them feel equal.

Chapter Conclusion

In conclusion, leadership is an integral part of human life. Leaders are present in families, in schools, in societies, in workplaces. What makes a person successful in this regard is his ability to challenge, create, achieve, inspire, energize, assess, and ultimately decide what is best for himself and his followers.

Finally, good leaders are made not born. Leadership is a skill and it can be developed from an early age.

Important Points to Note

- Identify areas of improvement for becoming an effective leader.
- Start taking ownership and initiatives in family, society and at the workplace.
- Improve public speaking, problem solving and decision-making skills.
- Keep reading and learning new things every day to expand your mind.

Decision-making Skills

"Whenever you see a successful business, someone once made a courageous decision."
— Peter F. Drucker

What Is Decision-making?

David started narrating a story to Henry and Jacob.

A kid walked into a big toy shop with his dad and was amazed by the array of toys on display.

"What should I select? What should I select? What should I select?" He asked himself.

"Come on son, be quick," his dad said.

"I like this one. No wait, I like this one."

He just couldn't make up his mind.

"Quick son, decide fast. We have to leave," His impatient father said.

The boy ran around the shop, his eyes oscillating from one shelf to another. He was so confused that he couldn't make a decision.

Eventually, the father lost his temper, grabbed his son by the arm and they walked out of the store empty-handed. The young boy had his eyes filled with tears. He wanted them all but ended up with nothing because he couldn't choose one.

The world is that toy shop. We are just like the boy. We have a myriad of options available to us, but if we don't decide at the right time about our career, education, relationships, investments, or other important issues, we end up empty-handed.

Why does it happen? Because we are too worried about taking the wrong decision.

But, the bigger danger is that we take no decision at all and end up doing nothing.

Everyone has difficulty in making decisions at times. People often say, "I just can't make up my mind!" Delay in taking decisions or the inability to take any decision is the biggest obstacle in your progress. Improving your decision-making skills can help you approach decisions with more confidence. Developing your decision-making abilities can give you more freedom and control over your life and increase your chances of being satisfied with your decisions. A skilled decision-maker develops more alternatives and is better equipped to choose the best from them.

Decision-making is the process of selecting one course of action from several alternative actions. To improve your decision-making skills, you need to know yourself, your values, and your abilities. Even in a situation with limited choices, decision-making is involved. Although many decisions are made largely by habit, others involve weighing two or more alternatives.

Why Is Decision-Making Important?

In today's competitive world, there is a tremendous need for good decision makers. People who have the ability to make decisions quickly and responsibly are needed in organizations. Since childhood, people take a lot of important decisions such as, "Should I study to become a doctor or a lawyer or an engineer? Should I focus on swimming or chess or tennis? Entire future of children depends on these decisions, and many people take these important decisions purely on impulse. This is why it is so important for you to learn good decision-making skills from early age itself.

People make numerous decisions every day. Many are easy and simple, but others are complex and stressful. Decision-making is one of the top priorities, and therefore, it is important to know how to improve it. Your decision-making process impacts overall work productivity and satisfaction.

The better you are at making decisions, the more success will you experience in your position. Demonstrating your decision-making skills at work can be beneficial when seeking higher leadership positions.

The Decision-Making Process

The steps in the decision-making process for any situation involving individual, organization, family, etc. are similar. These steps include:

1. *Know the problem or opportunity:* The decision-making process begins with recognizing a need for change.
2. *Analyze the situation:* Once you recognize that there is an opportunity, study the situation carefully. Try to find

the real cause and study potential opportunities.

3. *Consider the purpose:* You should understand the purpose you want to achieve. The purpose is influenced by your values and beliefs. You should learn how to select what is important from the information available.

4. *Look for alternatives:* You should look for as many alternatives as possible to solve your problem, not just the obvious ones. It will be worthwhile to spend more time and effort in identifying alternatives if the decision is very important.

5. *Study the consequences*: One of the key elements of the decision-making process is looking ahead to factor the risks. "What might happen if I do this!" Consider the use of resources, too: What resources are needed to carry out each alternative? How much time, energy, skill, money, knowledge, or other resources are required? What must be given up? Which

choice fits better with your values and goals? Writing down the answers to these questions helps to focus your thinking.

6. *Choose the best alternative*: You should look at the possible alternatives and select the one that seems best for you in terms of the purpose and the resources you have. None of the alternatives may be suitable for you. In this case, perhaps a new alternative can be created by modifying some of the alternatives.

7. *Execute the decision*: You must put your decision into action after choosing the best alternative.

8. *Accept responsibility:* You must accept the responsibility for the decision and the consequences. You should always plan to abide by your choice until changes or improvements are made to it. Most decisions are made under conditions of some uncertainty, imperfect knowledge, and limited resources.

9. *Evaluate the results:* You should evaluate the results of decisions to determine their effectiveness. All decisions should be reviewed periodically to ensure its effectiveness and suitability in the current situation.

How to Improve Decision-Making Skills

While everyone has to make decisions, it is surprising how little people know about making a good decision. Most decisions are made without any idea of the decision-making principles. With better decision-making skills, the percentage of correct decisions would improve.

- **Do Research**

You need to do detailed research on the subject. Try to get as much information as possible for better clarity. Once facts are ready, you will be able to gauge the pros and cons, and you will be able to take the decision accordingly.

- **Ask Questions**

When you ask repeated questions on the subject, things will unfold slowly and decision-making will become easier. These are some examples of the questions. "What do you feel about the decision? What do I expect? What is the purpose? Will the outcome of my decision help me to get what I truly want? What about the cost? What if the decision turns out to be wrong? Is the level of risk worth the reward? How committed am I for this decision?"

- **Follow Your Intuition**

When you have multiple options and your mind is oscillating between choices, your intuition is one of your most powerful decision-making tools. To hone in on your gut feeling, stop for a moment, sit in a quiet place and observe what feelings come into your mind.

Neuroscientist Dr. Joel Pearson discovered that intuition does exist and has demonstrated that unconscious emotions improve the speed and accuracy of decision-making.

When taking big decisions, you have got to tune into your inner wisdom. The best ancient advice for figuring out what you truly want is to look within.

- **Understand the Impact of Your Decision**

  Before you take a decision, you have to understand the effects of your choice. Any decision that you make causes a chain of events to happen. You need to understand all the probable impacts of each choice.

- **Align With Your Core Values**

  When decisions are taken based on your core values, they are motivationally aligned. It is always better to make decisions based on whether or not they are aligned with core values, passions, goals, and priorities.

Chapter Conclusion

Decision-making is one of the most important aspects of life and it has a direct impact on success. Decision-making can be quite tricky and challenging in some cases. Therefore, it is important to gather as much information as possible from different sources and evaluate all possible alternatives before making a decision. By doing this, you will be able to arrive at the best possible solution for the problem.

All successful people achieve their goals through effective and timely decision-making. The decision-making process is guided by beliefs, values, attitudes, knowledge, experiences, and availability of resources.

Important Points to Note

- Understand why decision-making process is important.
- Risk benefit analysis of each alternative and its impact should be assessed before taking decisions.

- Important elements for decision-making are proper research, questioning, availability of resources, intuition or gut feeling, etc.

Comprehensive Skill Matrix

Henry asked David, "You have taught us so many skills, but I am still confused about how they are interrelated."

David replied "To be good at problem solving, you need to have good analytical and communication skills also. Similarly, to have good problem solving skills, you need to be good at analyzing, communicating, etc."

"This is a bit confusing, David," said Henry.

"Henry, you are right. Many skills are interrelated. To enhance the overall skill set of your children, you should encourage them to start doing common things which will lead to improving all the skills. For example, Reading will improve all your skills, from writing to leadership."

"David, I do not understand what you are saying?" said Jacob.

David replied "You need to understand the inter-relation of skills with different activities. Then, accordingly, you can prioritize activities such as reading, writing, analyzing your speaking, etc. to be focused."

Table 1: Inter-relation of the different skills with activities

	Reading	Writing	Learning	Asking questions	Observation	Communication	Listening
Public speaking						*	
Writing	*	*	*				
Problem solving	*		*	*	*	*	*
Analytical	*		*	*	*		
Negotiation			*	*		*	*

	Reading	Writing	Learning	Asking questions	Observation	Communication	Listening
Leadership	*		*		*	*	*
Decision-making	*		*	*			*

* indicates the association of activities and corresponding skills.

The above template is an example of how activities are related to different skills. Certain activities such as reading, learning, listening have an impact on multiple skills. Hence, you should prioritize your learning activities in a way that maximize your benefits.

Skill Matrix (Self-Assessment)

Further, it is difficult to become an expert in all skills, but if you evaluate your total skill set, you will be able to know your overall current skill level. A person with at least 50% of the total skill set will be considered to have good skills and is more likely to be successful in life. It will also make you understand in which skills you are good at and in which skills you need to work. The Skills Matrix is a part of skills management. The primary goal of the skills matrix is to map all the skills and their status.

Table 2: Self-assessment matrix

Skills	Score				
	1 (NI)	2 (AV)	3 (GO)	4 (VG)	5 (EX)
Public speaking					
Writing					
Analytical					
Problem solving					
Negotiation					
Leadership					
Decision-making					
Score obtained					
Total Score	No. of Skills X Maximum individual score = 7 X 5 = 35				
% Score	Score obtained X 100 / Total Score				

(Notations: NI – Need Improvement, AV – Average, GO – Good, VG – Very Good, EX – Excellent)

Interpretation of Score:

During the self-assessment, you fill the above table based on understanding of your current level and find out the total score and percentage of total score obtained. If score obtained is more than 90%, your overall skill level is 'Excellent'. When score is between 70-90%, 50-70%, 30-50% and below 30%, your overall skill levels are 'Very Good', 'Good', 'Average' and 'Needs Improvement' respectively.

You can create skill matrices by using spreadsheets or making a chart. By this, you'll have a clearer picture of your actual skills and current skills, competences and areas of improvement. You can customize your skill matrix by adding all other general skills and subject-related skills.

Book Summary

Life is a journey. In this beautiful journey, people travel with different traits, some with sports, some with teaching, some with social services, but ultimately every person reaches a destination, knowingly or unknowingly.

This book has covered seven essential skills: public speaking, writing, analytical, problem solving, negotiation, leadership, and decision-making. These skills are important for everybody, especially for students who are trying to build the foundation of their future. There are many other skills, such as social skill, persuasion skill, and inspirational skill besides subject-specific skills, which also contribute to success but are not covered in this book. But, these seven tools are essential for success in life.

Public speaking is the key driver of success in life. It is useful in every facet of life. Effective public speaking skills can benefit students with career advancement, as they involve creativity, critical thinking skills, leadership abilities, and professionalism—qualities which are highly valuable for the career development. Speaking at events and conferences is a good way of building credibility. Public speaking can significantly boost your confidence. Your confidence levels will grow as you go from speaking to small groups of people to large audiences. This will benefit you not just on stage but in everyday life as well, whether it be in a meeting or on a date.

Sharpening your written communication skills can help you go a long way. Good grammar, structured content, story writing, editing, and better sentence construction are tools in the professional world to impress the audience, to build your network, and to work your way to the top. Good writing skills allow you to communicate your message with clarity and ease to a far larger audience than face-to-face or telephone conversations. The future belongs to those who can connect and communicate. Having excellent writing skills can make you an indispensable member of your team or company.

Analytical skills helps you to evaluate problems, both simple and complex. This skill incorporates many skills like attention to detail, critical thinking, decision-making, and research skills to analyze a question or problem and reach a solution.

Those with good problem solving skills are a valuable and trusted asset in any team – these are the people who think of new ideas, better ways of doing things, make it easier for people to understand things, or help save customers time and money.

Good negotiation skills contribute significantly to business success, as they help you build better relationships, deliver lasting and quality solutions rather than poor short-term solutions. Good negotiation skills help build relationships because the aim is to foster goodwill despite the difference in interests. Good negotiation skills also help in avoiding future conflicts and problems by leaving both parties equally satisfied with no barriers to communication for the future.

Leadership can benefit every aspect of your life, giving you greater confidence, strengthening your communication and negotiation skills, and developing your character. The values you learn as a leader can improve your personal life and relationships, setting you on the fast track to success in your professional and personal life.

The aptitude to make decisions is a leadership trait, which portrays your ability to think objectively and relate concepts to the goals you're trying to reach. Your capacity to make a quick decision can help establish a strong bond with all employees, which will strengthen your company's culture.

In a nutshell, this book has covered seven essential skills that will create the foundation for success in life. Working on these skills will significantly improve your qualities. The more you put these skills into practice in your daily life and work, the more you will be able to use them towards the achievement of your goals.

"No matter how talented you are, your talent will fail you, if you're not skilled. Skill is achieved through practice. Work hard and dedicate yourself to being better every single day." – Will Smith

Disclaimer

Although the publisher and the author have made every effort to ensure that the information in this book is correct, and while this publication is designed to provide accurate information regarding the subject matter covered, the publisher and the author assume no responsibility for errors, inaccuracies, omissions, or any other inconsistencies herein and hereby disclaim any liability to any party for any loss, damage, or disruption caused by errors or omissions, whether such errors or omissions result from negligence, accident, or any other cause.

The ideas, procedures, and suggestions contained in this book are not intended as a substitute for consulting with an expert. Neither the author nor the publisher shall be liable or responsible for any loss or damage allegedly arising from any information or suggestion in this book.

Names, characters, and incidents in this book are either the product of the author's imagination or used in a fictitious manner. Any resemblance to an actual person, living or dead, or actual events is purely coincidental.

Gratitude

I owe this book to my parents, from whom I imbibed my core values; all that I have, leads back to them. I am grateful to my better half and my son, whose continuous support and inspiration help me to continue on the writer's journey.

I sincerely thank all my readers, who inspired me with their love and appreciation for my first book.